W9-BDC-680

Things You'd Never Expect A Southerner To Say

Published by LONGSTREET PRESS, INC.,
a subsidiary of Cox Newspapers,
a subsidiary of Cox Enterprises, Inc.
2140 Newmarket Parkway
Suite 118
Marietta, Georgia 30067

Copyright © 1995 by

All rights reserved. No part of this book may be reproduced in any form by any means without
the prior written permission of the Publisher, excepting brief quotations used in connection with
reviews, written specifically for inclusion in a magazine or newspaper.

Printed in the United States of America

2nd printing, 1995

Library of Congress Catalog Number 95-77251

ISBN: 1-56352-239-X

Cover/jacket design by Neil Hollingsworth

Things You'd Never Expect A Southerner To Say

by
Vic Henley

illustrations by
Ron Bell

LONGSTREET PRESS
Atlanta, Georgia

To
J.P. WILLIAMS
A creative genius, no matter what anyone says.

Special thanks to the following: Robin Henley, Jeff Foxworthy, Jeffery "Buzz" Sutherland, the Rothwells, the Murphrees, and Phil "Alone in the Wilderness" King. Without you I am nothing.

Foreword

What is it about the Southern accent? Others hear it and automatically they want to deduct 100 I.Q. points. I know this because I've traveled the country and I've been told I have somewhat of an accent. However, compared to Vic I sound like I'm from New Hampshire.

I remember visiting Vic once when he lived in New York City. During the week he had other friends from Alabama drop in. As we were walking down Broadway, one of his childhood cronies looked into a store window and hollered, "Whooowee! What do you reckon something like that cost?" We grabbed him by the arm and under our breath said, "Keep your mouth shut until we get home!" We were young in our comedy careers and couldn't afford the robbery that surely would have occurred had anyone heard the group of us talking.

I recall another night in Chicago when Vic, inspired by a couple of canned beverages, climbed on top of a sofa in a hotel room located on the 40th floor. He threw his arms out and in a voice that originated deep in his sinuses proclaimed, "Chi town, my town!"

The point being, "Southern" is a beautiful language. Those not blessed at birth to be able to speak it may scoff at it, and that's okay. But they're going to be real surprised when they get to heaven and Saint Peter says, "Get in the truck, we're going up to the big house."

One thing you'll never hear a Southerner say is that Vic Henley ain't funny. I guarantee it.

— **Jeff Foxworthy**

Croquet, anyone?

The two-step is just too difficult.

I feel as if I'm about to regurgitate.

We don't keep firearms in this house.

It's time to stop fishing;
we've caught our limit.

Let's wash the car.

I just can't wait for that Fellini festival.

Ed Koch seems like a swell fellow.

Has anybody seen the sideburn trimmer?

Come to think of it, I'll have a Heineken.

You can't feed that to the dog.

That's enough ketchup
on those eggs.

I thought Graceland was tacky.

Don't worry, I've got a spare in the trunk.

No kids in the back of the pickup!

We're out of Balsamic vinegar.

Alex, I'll take Shakespeare for $1000.

Let's change the sheets.

Wrasslin's fake.

Things You'd Never Expect A Southerner To Say

My wife and I are going shopping for wallpaper.

I like pine nuts in my pasta.

That Civil War documentary was excellent.

Let's leave the kids at home.

I think communists are backing
the NRA.

That aroma? I'm baking fresh bagels.

55 is a reasonable speed limit.

Hold the grits, please.

No, I better not have another cold beer.

Good heavens, that's gaudy!

Let's stop and fill up. We don't have but a quarter of a tank.

I'm putting this money into a savings account.

Honey, did you mail that contribution to Greenpeace?

It just can't be fixed.

I wouldn't know how to throw
a horseshoe.

We better check with the union first.

We're vegetarians.

Do you think my hair is too big?

I've got a problem with people who still fly the Confederate flag.

Pavoratti is my favorite tenor.

Here are my keys.
I'm too drunk to drive.

Leave the dog outside.

How do you use these jumper cables?

Yachting is much more fun
than fishing.

Baby, those jeans are too tight.

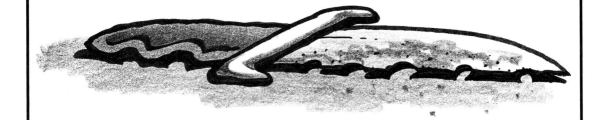

That buck knife's too rusty.

I'll have grapefruit
instead of biscuits and gravy.

Honey, these bonsai trees
need watering.

Call your mama and see if she wants
to go with us.

Nobody in our family drinks.

Let me pay this time.

Don't tie it on top of the car.

My mama can't make cornbread.

What's a taxidermist?

Does two pair beat three of a kind?

Who's Richard Petty?

Give me the small bag of pork rinds.

Those truffles were stale.

Hold still while I zoom in.

Deer heads detract from the decor.

I'm sorry I'm so loud.

Spitting is such a nasty habit.

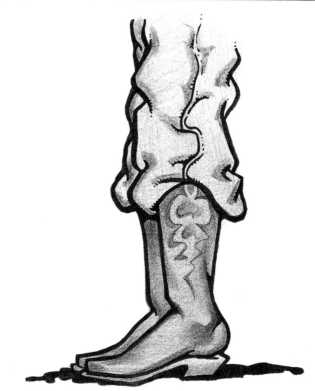

These boots hurt my feet.

I prefer to grind my own coffee.

Bowling alleys should close earlier.

I hate the long version of "Freebird."

I just couldn't find a thing
at Wal-Mart today.

I've never bounced a check for livestock.

What's Hank Jr.'s last name?

Trim the fat off that steak.

Cappuccino tastes better than *espresso*.

Why'd you cut the sleeves off your t-shirt?

The tires on that truck are too big.

I have finally found a good psychiatrist.

Making bail should be no problem.

I'll have the arugula and radicchio salad.

Don't spray primer there.

I've got it all on floppy disk.

Would you like your fish poached or broiled?

NASCAR racing is just
one long left turn.

Unsweetened tea tastes better.

My fiancée, Paula Jo, is registered at Tiffany's.

Put that dog on a leash.

Mama has no opinion on that.

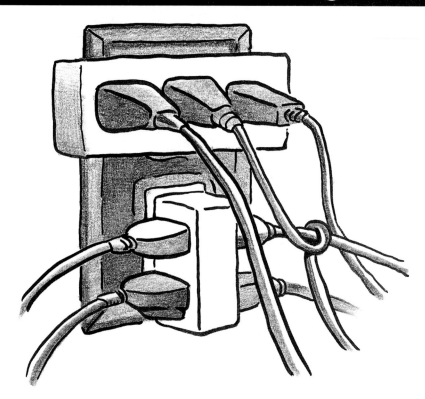

Careful, that may be a fire hazard.

Let's mow the lawn.

New York City is an ideal place
to vacation.

Let's not tailgate before the game.

Lisa Marie was lucky
to snag Michael Jackson.

My mobile home's clean
and storm proof.

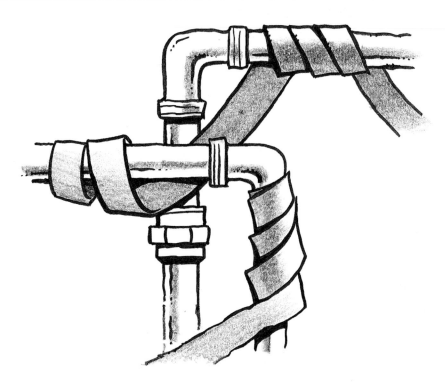

Duct tape won't fix it.

I'm a Shiite Muslim.

I don't want a flannel shirt
for Christmas.

I've got two cases of Zima
for the Super Bowl.

Yes, I realize that I'm suppressing my inner child.

Jimmy, get in here quick — the Boston Marathon's on Channel 2!

Wouldn't Brenda love a subscription
to *Gourmet* magazine for Christmas?

Little Debbie snack cakes
have too many fat grams.

Grandma only smokes Cuban cigars.

Checkmate.

She's too old
to be wearing that bikini.

Y'all hiring?

Does the salad bar have bean sprouts?

Hey, here's an episode of "Hee Haw"
we haven't seen.

I'm overdue for a pedicure.

I don't have a favorite college team.

I only smoke menthol.

You think I've got too many beer lights in my game room?

Daddy hates shooting pool.

Lord, I'm sick of hearing "Dixie."

Who's that guy that wrote
Gone with the Wind?

Mama, don't paint the poodle's toenails. It looks silly.

Anybody want some pop?

I believe you cooked those green beans too long.

It's an excellent coffee-table book.

Aren't you going to recycle that?

If it's a girl, we're gonna name her for Margaret Thatcher.

Those shorts ought to be
a little longer, Darla.

Kudzu makes an excellent ground cover.

I wouldn't drive an American make
if you paid me.

We've never received an overdue notice.

Let's watch *Smokey and the Bandit*
on laser disk.

Elvis who?

What does that mean, "Fergit, hell!"?

Those Monster Truck Show tickets
are too expensive.

It's too big.

You can't take that tractor on
the blacktop.

I really admire Teddy Kennedy.

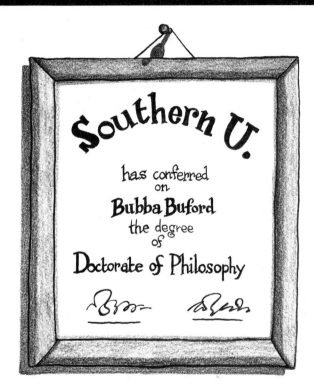

Southern U.

has conferred
on
Bubba Buford
the degree
of
Doctorate of Philosophy

Where'd you get your doctorate?

The homeowner's policy is paid in full.

That's not Ed's junk out in the yard. It's folk art.

Be sure to bring my salad dressing on the side.

I ain't riding with you unless both headlights work.

That movie won "Best Picture" at Cannes.

It's January — take the Christmas lights down.

Fishing's just a waste of time.

Baling wire won't hold it.

The mosquitoes aren't bad in August.

Granny was a Rhodes Scholar.

I'm raising free-range chickens.

Just a second, Irene, I'm going to pull
over and check the map.

It's the humidity, not the heat.

I'm using new tin on the roof.

That was a stupid article in *Field and Stream*.

All country music sounds the same.

The fish weren't biting today.

What's on "Masterpiece Theatre" this evening?